Mosaic

A Collection

Pam Collings

Published by Pam Collings

Copyright © Pam Collings 2020

 A catalogue record for this work is available from the National Library of Australia

ISBN 978-0-9923002-8-9 (pbk)

The Author of this book accepts all responsibility for the contents and absolves any other person or persons involved in its production from any responsibility or liability where the contents are concerned.

All rights reserved. No part of this publication may be reproduced, stored in a retrieval system, or transmitted, in any form, by any means, electronic, mechanical, photocopying, recording or otherwise, without prior permission from the author.

Typeset in Garamond 11pt

Produced by **TB Books**
        P.O. Box 8138
        Seymour South Victoria 3660 Australia
        Email: tbbooks@collings.id.au

Cover Design by Pam Collings

Contents

Introduction 7
Autumn Leaves 9
Abandoned 10
Accounting 11
Bright Points 12
Donkey's Years 13
Destiny Amongst Us 14
Faulty Existence 16
Dog's Breath 21
Beating the Abyss 23
Feeling Good 25
Dragon 26
Dark to Light 28
Calling No Fear 29
Forgotten 32
Gaining Acceptance 33
Gaps Between Time 34
Jigsaw Puzzle 36
Words 37
Lingering 38
Driven 39
Haiku Diatribe 40
    I 40
    II 40
    III 40
    IV 40
    V 40
    VI 41
Magic in the Air 42
Feathers 43
Bubbles 45
The Black Hole 46
Little Voices 48
Illusion 50
Cleaning Up 51
Eclipse 53

Memory # 2	54
Mimic	55
Expanse	57
Moments Like These	59
In the Semi Dark	61
Music in my Mind	62
Looking Forward to Peace	63
Afterwards	65
Fairy Tale – Not	66
Hidden in the Mists	67
Maze	68
Relaxing	70
Ring of Fire	71
Fearsome Creatures	73
It's time	75
Miracle	76
They Call Me Numbat	77
Midnight	79
Child of Mine	81
Devil's Edge	82
Energy	83
Misty	84
No Explanation	85
Glimpses	86
Powerball	88
Recollections	89
Crystal Ball	90
Philosophy	92
Sleepy Head	94
The Locker Door	96
The Wind	98
Haze	100
Finding the Future	101
Sunshine	104
Starbright	105
Springlike	106
Time Jumping	108
Wizard Fire	110
Procrastination	112
The Sign	113

The Short Straw 114
Night Time 115
Perception 116
Conviction 118
Bonfire 119
Floating 120
The Bench 122
Changes 124
Drip 125
Watching Time 127
Musical Life 129
Mosaic 130
The Author 131
Other Books by Pam Collings 132
    Soon to be released: 132

Introduction

This is my second anthology of poetry. I hope you like it.

You will find within these covers a collection of diverse poetry - some serious, some quirky, some cute. They are mostly snapshots of my life and always about the emotions of that particular moment or event. Although sometimes I just decided to pick a subject and write a poem about it. As I said - diverse.

Poetry to me is all about emotion, without it, it is just not poetry.

Even if you are not into poetry, I'd like to think that there is something in these pages for everyone to enjoy and understand.

If you missed my first anthology, *Kaleidoscope*, and you would like to check it out, you can contact me for a copy. It is also available from Amazon or Book Depository in both paperback and e-book format.

Thank you for reading!

Autumn Leaves

The air cools
The wind crisps
The leaves crumble
And fall.

The ground is bathed
In orange and lemon,
As the days pass,
Souring to browns.

Beneath the crunching,
A soft layer
Of inner warmth
Reaches out.

Until the air warms,
The wind mellows,
And the leaves,
Grow.

Abandoned

As the tears fall,
They are replaced
By hollowness
So deep,
The whole world
Could be swallowed.

Flickering shadows
Live within,
Aching to escape
The abyss
Of hopelessness.

There's no bell
To toll here,
No sense of here
At all really.

Existence is futile.

As the tears fall,
They are replaced
By more tears.

Followed by waiting.

Hopeless waiting.

Accounting

One plus one equals zero,
Four minus one equals zero,
Two multiplied by one equals zero,
Thirty-five divided by two equals zero.

Nothing adds up anymore.

The calculator is broken,
The accountant is sick,
And the fingers are full of arthritis,

Nothing counts anymore,

But I've always hated numbers,
Maths is boring,
Accountants play with the numbers
Of our lives.

Nothing equals zero.

And zero doesn't count.

Not when I'm NUMBER ONE.

Bright Points

Bright points
of light
march off
into the distance.

Hypnotic
thoughts float
unbidden
in a lost mind.

The distance
marches off
into a future
of uncertainty.

Only time
knows what
lies ahead
on that dark road.

Sometimes
the foot
eagerly
presses forward.

But then
no!
it eases
almost to a stop.

Concentration wanes
on the onward
track,
carelessness prevails.

Donkey's Years

It feels like ages,
Like everything
Is drawn out,
Like mozzarella cheese
On a pizza.

Reluctant to completely
Break free,
But inevitably
Forced to do so.

It's definitely
3 steps forward,
2 steps backward,
Although mostly
It feels like
3 steps forward,
4 steps back.

We must believe
That progress is being made,
Look to solve one obstacle
At a time,
And make each turning point
A celebration,
As we build towards our climax.

It will happen.
And then our denouement
Will come.

It's a pity it's taken donkey's years.

Destiny Amongst Us

Swirling, swaying
Through the
Emptiness of my mind.

Weaving and waving
Around the recesses
Of my heart.

Taking my life for granted.

Where no one lives,
No one dies,
When no one tries,
No one can fail.

The thoughts
Keep returning,
Battering against
The brick wall
Of my will.

Settling into a pool
Of uselessness,
Until the pit
Of stubbornness
Opens and devours me.

But I rise again,
And again,
And again.

Pushed by destiny
To succeed,
Even when success
Seems futile.

That's the strange
Thing about destiny -
It always prevails

One
Way
Or
Another.

Destiny is as destiny does.

Creating our ultimate happiness.

Faulty Existence

The darkness
Lifts a fraction,
Eyes struggle to open,
The crack between the lids
Barely large enough
To sense the beginning
Of another day.

An alarm,
Loud and shrill
In the morning brightness,
Then silence descends,
As a hand lurches out
And swipes the clock
Dead.

The cracked eyelids
Descend again into darkness,
The mind blurs
Into dreams,
Nondescript,
Indistinct,
Part only of the sleeping world.

Until
The radio blares to life,
Alarming the morning
Once again,
But barely making an impression
Upon the exhausted
Slumbering consciousness.

The news arrives,
And a buried spark
Of awareness
Struggles to rise
Above the cloying
Darkness of sleep,
To listen to the worthiness of the day.

It misses the highlights,
Skips the traffic reports,
Zones into report #1,
Zones out for report #2,
Catches numbers 3 and 4,
Forgets the sport,
And barely catches the weather.

A sigh escapes,
It's time,
To rise
To the day ahead,
To wake others,
Make lunches,
Send them off to their day

Legs swing
Over the side of the bed,
They dangle,
Waiting for instructions,
When they don't come
From the numb brain,
They move of their own accord.

Mosaic

Upright now,
Moving hesitantly
Forward,
Making the motions,
The morning rituals
Begin on auto pilot.

The house is empty now,
It's time to work,
To begin the day
That belongs
To the body and mind
Itself,
And no one else.

The computer alights,
Emails are read, answered
Automatically,
Desk re-arranged,
Files opened
Ready
To be worked upon.

Must be morning tea,
The kettle boils,
A snack of biscuit and cheese
Arranged upon the plate,
The lot settles into the couch,
Crunching the biscuits,
Sipping of tea,
Minutes pass.

After an hour,
The hands push
The body from the cushions,
And the legs propel
Back to the computer,
Emails are checked again,
And then the eyes stare at the screen.

Suddenly it's time,
To pick up others,
Only half an hour
Of work so far.

A hand passes across
Weary eyes,
Lethargic,
Rises to go.

An extra effort
Is tried on return,
Another half hour
Is dredged from the computer,
The temporary activity
Dims again,
As the mind slumps into weariness once more.

Dinner is wrought,
Slamming through
The lethargy
Of the day
So poorly spent,
A day where sleep only
Is the drawcard.

Mosaic

As night descends,
And TV beckons,
The mind starts,
To waken to guilt,
It decides to try once more
To complete the tasks
That it must.

But it doesn't last long,
The body refuses to respond
To the commands to act,
It stays rooted to its seat,
Comfortable,
Drifting,
Weary.

Weary from nothing,
As if breathing alone
Is too much,
The mind recognises
This as unnatural,
The question asked

What is the problem?

But there is no answer,
Not immediately forthcoming,
For now the mind and body
Must just struggle to function,
They must overcome the hurdle,
They must survive,
Survival is everything.

One day it will change.

The heart hopes so, at least.

Dog's Breath

Lying on the floor,
Minding my own business,
Spot wags his tail in my face.

Stop that, Spot, I yell.

He stops,
Then plops himself
Across my legs,
A dead weight
That quickly turns
My legs to mush.

Get off, Spot, I yell.

He jumps up,
And walks around,
And around,
And around,
Where I'm lying
On the floor,
Trying to have some peace.

Sit down, Spot, I yell.

He sits,
Right in front of my face,
And then he leans forward,
And licks me from chin to hair,
A happy grin upon his muzzle,
Tongue hanging out,
Panting hot fetid breath.

Mosaic

I can't be angry
When he looks like that.

I reach up and hug him.

I love you, too, Spot, I whisper.

Beating the Abyss

Toes pressed to the edge,
I spread my arms wide,
Eyes glued to
The black expanse before me.

I rock back and forth,
With ever increasing force,
Waiting for the moment
When I will topple

Into the black abyss.

But it goes on forever,
So long
That fingers of blackness
Reach up and wrap around me.

They try to pull me
Down and over
Into the think syrupy
Void.

But they fail,
Even as my toes
Lose their grip
On the edge.

And I stumble
Forward
A scream
Ripping from me.

Mosaic

To be replaced
By a 'What the?'
Of surprise.

Above the abyss
Wooden slats
Of a narrow bridge
Form as I step out.

One foot in front of the other,
One slat at a time,
As,
Arms still outstretched,
I move forward.

Crossing the danger,
Of the black abyss,
Escaping the clutches,
Of its darkness.

Abandoning its call.

Now I'm looking up
Instead of down,
Moving forward
Instead of teetering.

Still unsure
But at least not hopeless.

Feeling Good

Everything's fine,
In my life right now,
It's rolling along happily,
I'm not sure how.

I wake up every day,
To a bird's happy song,
Whether he's singing or not,
Nothing seems to be wrong

Oh, sometimes there'll be moments,
That aren't really all that great,
But in the greater scheme of things
Life's been good to me of late.

My wishing and my wanting,
Have been for things to be
Working and running smoothly,
To the best of their ability.

Past wishes for riches,
Or good luck for all things sweet,
Is, at the moment,
Tucked away all nice and neat.

Life is pretty good to me,
And I hope it stays that way,
I'll certainly be trying hard to keep it so,
Each and every day.

Dragon

Behind closed eyes,
A mind, open and excited
Chases rainbows,
Across the blackness.

Until …

It roars to life,
Huge leather wings,
Beating hot waves
Of air down upon the land.

Then …

It spies you,
Flames ignite its jaws,
Wings beat against
The updraft,
And it falls.

When …

It lands,
You cringe,
Trying to make yourself,
As small
As possible,
So it doesn't know you're there.

But …

It sees you,
It smells you,
It senses you,

It somehow hears you.

Maybe your heartbeat
Gives you away.

And ...

It springs,
Knocking you to the ground,
Straddling your shaking
Body,
And bends its head

To ...

Lick you from chin
To forehead,
Tail wagging,
Tongue panting.

So ...

You laugh and spring
To your feet,
Reaching up to embrace
Your pet dragon ...

Claude.

Dark to Light

The empty canvass,
The loaded brush,
A heavy heart
Poured forth.

With darkness shaded.

The brush dips again,
The canvass glows,
In the upper right hand corner,
Reaching back to the depth

Coaxed into shadows.

Across the board,
The spray of light,
Reaches out to scatter
The particles of night.

Shyly dreaming of the light.

Paint, in pastels,
Light and airy

Streak across the surface
Banishing the dark.

Beaming freely is the Joy

Again.

Calling No Fear

I'm tired
No longer want
To fight
Or compromise

No more

I surrender

I give in

I agree

It's time
To move on
To find
Life worth being

It's right
To put a stop
To the past

To forge a new future

In the meantime

This no man's land
We're in
Creates confusion
Births loneliness
Expounds hopelessness

Mosaic

Until there is nothing
But fear

To just know
What tomorrow
Might bring

To really know
That the future
Will hold

Lightness
And wonder
And joy

To be sure
That life
Will indeed
Be better
Be as it really should be

Enable dreams
To be fulfilled

Bring appreciation
And caring

The universe gives us what we need

Do unto others
But bitterness rises
And revenge
Does sound sweet

Until fear steps in
Turns thoughts away

If only there were no fears
But there is

And that's how it needs to be

The universe wins again.

Forgotten

Time stands still
   Waters swirl
      In the evening breeze.

Winds dance through the trees
   Singing the praises
      Of the forgotten secrets.

Shorthand promise
   Steals the joy
      From the inner soul.

Memories of spring
   Temper the fever
      Of a summer's fire.

Nothing exists beyond
   The universe embraces all
      The life within.

Gaining Acceptance

Like a tree
Reaching
Towards
The sun

The knowledge slowly grows

Like the water
Welling
Within
The earth

The calm seeps within.

Like the breeze
Rustling
Through
The branches

The emotions turn from fear

To bitterness
To confusion
To resentment tinged with hate.

Until finally
Acceptance steps in
And a breath of fresh air
Shows how everything can be

Better

The way it should be.

Gaps Between Time

In the gaps
Between time
Life takes a rest

As it rests
Peace
Lights the world

Lit from within
The world
Spins with delight

In the gaps
Between time

When the mists descend
Mystery begins
Shrouding everyday life

With life hidden
Away from prying eyes
Freedom breaks its bounds

Free from the world
Life spreads and breathes
Mutating into joy.

In the gaps
Between time.

Joy prances and frolics
To unheard music
In all the corners of the world

Music is born
Singing praise and wonder
In a manner beyond belief.

Belief in all things
Is created
From the mystery and the music.

In the gaps
Between time.

Emotion springs
From the life let free
Stirring senses dormant.

No longer dormant
Sensation blossoms
And dances to the music of time.

We are

Free from the shackles
Dancing with the joy
To the music of our senses.

In the gaps
Between time.

Jigsaw Puzzle

The jigsaw puzzle
Of life
I've never been much good
At jigsaw puzzles.

I can find the corners
And sometimes the edges
Make themselves found
But the inner bits ...

Well, that's just often too hard.

A hand reaches out
Touches mine
And I shy back
My mind a jigsaw of emotion.

The pieces scatter
Hide from me in the far
Reaches of my brain
Until my efforts stumble to a halt.

I touch and stroke
Leaving pieces of myself
To be found
But it seems to the wrong
Jigsaw

And then I wake one day
And the picture is complete.

Just not the me
I thought it to be.

Words

Words –
Visual representations
Of thoughts

Thoughts –
Insubstantial rationalisations
Of emotions

Emotions –
Abstract results
Of experiences

Experiences –
Kaleidoscopic scenes
Of events

Events –
Comprising climaxes
In the subplots

Of life

Subplots –
Building the plot
Of our lives

Described
By words.

Lingering

There's a soft hint of the flavour of him
Lying beside my pillow.

As I look about the room
There's evidence of his existence.

His aroma lingers upon
The surface of the furniture.

He is there, even if I can't see him.

My thoughts keep turning restlessly
Towards the one who is not here.

My curiosity wonders what he does now.
My dreams are haunted by images.

Lingering
Softly
Dancing
Blithely

Around the corners of my heart
Until my frustration grows, becomes a wild thing.

As everything lingering becomes intangible
And simply drifts away

From me, standing here all alone
And the violins play a haunting, lingering melody.

Driven

Driven beyond the want
To the need,
To do something I love,
But that is difficult.

Oh, so, difficult.

Ripping the words from within,
Where they lay buried,
But impatient
To break free.

Yet afraid to risk the light.

Hesitating to fill the dream,
Because failure
Would be so devastating,
So it's easier not to do.

Sometimes, easier, but not fulfilling.

The need pushes,
The want pulls,
The heart yearns,
But the mind prevents.

The life of a writer,

Where only two words count.

DO IT!

Haiku Diatribe

I

Empty mind
Purpose strong
Pushing towards creation.

II

Posing questions
Awaiting answers
An eternity passes by.

III

Eyes staring
Till itchy noses
Topple the hand of time.

IV

Ears twitching
Silence deafening
Lands a drop of sound.

V

Sensations tasting
Indefinable, indescribable,
Lost in the maze of time.

VI

Sleepy now
Pen drooping
Snores resonate, breathing hesitant.

Magic in the Air

Angel wings brush gently
Across my face,
The gentle breeze sighs
Blissfully,
Surrounding me with calm,
Persuading me with magic.

It speaks
Its language not my own,
But one I know I must learn,
The magic is important,
The magic sparkles.

It flickers on and then off,
The patterns too fast,
Too intricate,
For my mere human mind,
The sounds too complex
For my ear drums to interpret.

Yet ...

The magic weaves itself
About me,
Cocooning me in a nest
So strong and so safe
There is no need for anything else.

The magic lives,
The magic breathes,
The magic
Is me.

Feathers

Wisps of thoughts,
And touches of dreams,
Feather through the darkness,
Rippling as they go.

Catching on burrs,
And burrowing down deep,
They float and they dance,
Tantalising, bewildering.

Behind in their wake,
Vague notions of doubt,
Prod their way,
Until nothing is sure.

Certainty becomes cloudy,
The window of hope grimed,
The shadows flow deeply,
And the ghosts of fear revive.

Feathers of dreams,
And whispers of thought
Descend, return and breathe
Life back again

Into lifeless beliefs,
Brushing aside ungrounded fears,
Chasing away untimely concerns,
Blowing away the dust

Mosaic

Of settling apprehension.

Restoring a balance.

While faith flutters in to add strength.

Determination.

Hope.

Our thoughts, our worst enemy?

Our thoughts build salvation?

Anything is possible.

Our thoughts make it so.

Bubbles

Bubbles
Chasing rainbows
In the sun.

Shadows
Multicoloured
Upon the walls.

Tickling
Little noses
As they burst upon the tip.

Bubbles
Surfacing
In the ringlets of time.

Dancing
Upon the midnight
Darkness of the pool.

Popping
With a gaiety
A merriment of life.

Bubbles
Seeking truth
Finding wisdom on the wind.

The Black Hole

Out in front
Before me
A dark mass
Accumulates

And laughs

But I laugh back.

Stretching as far
As I can see
Silent, yet loud

The black hole

Beckons to me – unknown
Until now – frightening

In hindsight
Every moment
Of future
Is unknown
Impenetrable blackness

But I have met it
Tamed it
Made it part of me
Allowed myself
To learn and grow

To embrace it.

Until no fear remains

Because

It is no longer
Unknown
No longer anything
To fear

Because

It is my life
Familiar
Somewhat comfortable

But never the same.

The future
Is no scarier now
Than it ever has been

It is just different

Challenging

Something to explore
Maybe battle and conquer

Just something else
To become part of me

Life…

Little Voices

Little voices
Dance
Before my eyes.

Whispering
Brightly,
Lightly touching

With
Feather soft
Tendrils

The edges
Of the misty
Beginnings

Of emotionless
Depths
In the dark.

Little voices
Push
Away

The blanket
Of hesitancy,
Cuddling

Around
My heart
Beating slowly

Onward
Towards oblivion,
Until

The little voices
Trickle through
To open

My soul
To a reality
I fear.

Little voices
Fade, yet
Their power remains.

Illusion

Time stands still
While life rushes by
Pushing its silent noise
Behind it.

I stand alone amongst
This whirlpool of humanity
And watch as one by one
Each joins up.

Time stands still.
There is only me,
Only me waiting,
For the motion to begin.

God's heaven
Has gone to hell,
And he's waiting
For someone to save him.

Time stands still.
Orbits move to oblivion.
Darkness is nowhere.
Nowhere is light.

Time stands still.
The beginning ends again.
Life is dead.

Tell me – is this real?

Cleaning Up

Open the cupboard
And look inside,
What do you see?
What is trying to hide?

Is the chocolate
Beside the chocolate cake,
Or underneath
The things to bake.

Wherever you find it
Eat it up quick,
Because the day after tomorrow
It will be given the flick.

Along with the biscuits
The cakes and the slices,
They'll all be left
To their own woeful devices.

There'll be no more lollies
And no more fruit cake,
No more scones
Sweet or savoury to bake.

The time to right
Your health problems has come
It has to be now
Or there'll be no saving of some.

The light has lit up
The writing on the wall,
Get fit and get healthy
Or this might be all.

Mosaic

There may be no tomorrow
Let alone Tuesday week,
If some changes are not made
In a manner strong, not meek.

It's time to stop fighting
And to do what you must,
Whether you like it or not
Don't be stupid or fussed.

This time next year
There'll be a much better you,
Standing toe to toe
With your mirrored view.

So get up off your bum
And start right away,
To make you all better
Each and every new day.

Eclipse

Behind the sun
Lies the moon,
Shadowed,
Mysterious,
Even now.

Armstrong
Placed one
Foot in front
Of the other,
And declared
Words that
No one actually heard.

If only life
Was as simple
As a lunar eclipse.

But it isn't.

Instead we look up
Through the darkness
Of space,
And dream
Of a simpler
Existence.

Where love does not exist.

Memory # 2

The sound woke me,
Four o'clock in the a.m.,
Clip clop, clip clop,
A plod, half asleep.

The milk man cometh.

It was like rain
On a tin roof,
Comforting,
Soothing.

Welcoming the new day.

It was a memory
In the making,
For even though I hated milk
The milko was not to be.

Not for too much longer.

So I lay on my back,
Eyes closed, nose to the ceiling,
Ears drinking in the delicious,
Tones of the hard hooves on bitumen.

Savouring every last echo.

Of the soon to be bygone memory.

Mimic

Refrains of recently heard songs
Flow effortlessly
Through the dark corners
Of my thoughts.

Bouncing back
Time and again
To repeat themselves
Seemingly endlessly.

Competing, too,
Are the shadows
Lurking among
My thoughts.

One dimensional,
Detail free
Playing tag with
A soul of solitude.

The silvered glass
Stares back at me,
Its contents unrecognisable
From my thoughts.

A familiar stranger
Hung about with trappings,
Unwanted, unworthy,
A shell with no one inside.

Mosaic

Memories surface,
Play out across
The stage of my mind,
Re-enact times in my thoughts.

Been there, done that,
Deja vu,
Bags packed with emotion,
Echoes.

Expanse

Gaze upwards
Towards the bright lights
Of night.

Wonder,
Does anyone gaze
Back at me?

Millions of miniscule
Nebula
Shine down.

I must be
One of millions
Shining down on someone else.

Questions crowd me,
Revolving around me
Like moons about this earth.

There must be at least
One other
Like me

With trees and mountains,
Streams and seas,
Animals and man.

Without another,
Why should I exist?

Perhaps it's time to supanova.

Perhaps become

Mosaic

A black hole
In time.

Across the expanse
A bright flare
Is seen.

The one
Feels hope.

There are others.

Moments Like These

There're bubbles in my heart,
Rising as laughter in my throat,
To sit as a smile on my lips.
Contentment drapes itself
Around my shoulders,
Warming my soul.

Nestling in between my toes

Until the corners of my existence

Are filled.

It's moments like these
That life searches for,
Moments of happiness,
Moments of contentment,
Moments of joy.

Even a few of these
Moments
Seeking us out,
Keeping us whole,
Makes life meaningful.

The dark times,
The sad times,
The times of grief,
All fade away
In the light of brilliance
Shed by moments like these.

Mosaic

I can't wait for the next one
To appear around the corner
To surprise me,
Perhaps even shock me.

But always to fulfil
Me,
To fulfil a need I have,
To erase
The dark moment

And lift me
To heights I thought
I would never see again.

Reminding me that
If I open myself to them

They will come again.

And the more they come
The more I will open myself

To moments like these.

In the Semi Dark

In the semi dark
Of the light
Of a torch

I scratch away
At these words

Squeezed into being
In a corridor of dreams
Daddy long legs
For company
Nearby.

The glow of the light
Through the window
Next door
Adorns the clutter
Against the wall.

Leaving empty
My heart
As it beats a tattoo
Of wonder
And acceptance
Of all.

In the semi dark
I scratch at the words
As the torch light fades
To dusk.

Music in my Mind

The music in my mind,
Notes of varied colours,
With moods dancing,
As it circles around,
The centre of my existence.

The music in my mind,
Reminds me
Of times forgotten,
Times of memory,
As it strays within my existence.

The music in my mind,
Sways to a rhythm
All its own,
Taking its time to settle,
Within the realms of my existence.

The music in my mind,
Ever present, ever mine,
Never leaves me
As it ebbs and flows,
Amongst the clouds of my existence.

The music in my mind,
Keeps me sane,
Centres my soul and spirit,
As it nurtures my existence.

Without it, I cease to be.

Looking Forward to Peace

I feel like I'm floating,
Brushing gently against
The atmosphere.

Bouncing harmlessly
Off the edges
Of my existence.

Bending,
Pliable to the changes,
Malleable.

Constantly changing,
Adapting,
Accepting.

Heading towards
I know not where,
But moving forwards
All the same.

Sometimes I feel fear
Leak through to the surface
To poison my thoughts.

To upset my equilibrium.
But fear is born of ignorance,
Fear is born of inflexibility.

Fear is born of attachment
When sometimes that
Attachment
Is not healthy.

Mosaic

When sometimes
That attachment
Is not good for anyone.

When sometimes that
Attachment
Needs to be severed.

To allow the soul
To float free
And be all it can be,
And more.

When being free
Brings ultimate happiness,
Fulfilment of a soul
Starved and restricted
For too long.

A soul that needs more
Than just contentment.

It needs to risk, to feel, to be alive,
To create – life and meaning,
To fulfil destinies
That have waited
And feared they would never
Be fulfilled.

But destiny must be fulfilled.

Somehow.

Some way.

Always in time.

For destiny is the power of life.

Afterwards

Can't wait,
Can't wait,
Not any longer.

Afterwards
Has to come now
Has to come
So I can move on.

So I can be happy
Again
So life is not held captive
To a ransom
Too expensive
For even
Mr Rockerfeller.

It's time
To go
To move on
To end this hell.

Even if moving on
Leads to another hell.

This time it will be chosen
Not forced upon
Not stupidly insisted on.

This time it will be mine.

Fairy Tale – Not

Once upon a time
There was nothing,
No problems, no sadness,
No anger, no resentments.

Just cool contentment,
Happiness and understanding.

Then the Big Bang
Destroyed life as we know it.
Debris spread far
And confusion reigned.

Joy left by the back door,
Pain crept in through the front.

The heavens revolved,
And swayed round and round,
In time with the confusion,
And uncertainty.

It was never ending,
Never evolving.

It just floated
From side to side
And up and down,
Not able to settle comfortably.

Until they all lived
Happily Never After.

Hidden in the Mists

The veils of mist
Keep swirling
Left and right,
Backwards and forwards

Never still
Always moving

Promising to part
To reveal that which lies
Within,
But it never does.

At least not yet.

The mist enshrouds,
And surrounds,
Fingers itself through my hair,
Invades my nostrils,
Strips my eyes of sight,
Glues itself to my skin.

But it shows me nothing,
Just keeps dancing – and dancing.

Hiding everything
From plain sight.

Maze

Finding pathways
Round the obstacles
Life throws in front,
Walls moving
To prevent backtracking.

Can't see over,
Can't crawl under,
Can't go back,
Can only go forward.

Twisting to go this way,
Turning to go that,
Forcing through the frustration
Of dead ends and forgotten alleyways.

Can't see over,
Can't crawl under,
Can't go back,
Can only go forward.

Tears of frustration,
From failed thoughts of peace,
Determination building,
Determination fading.

Can't see over,
Can't crawl under,
Can't go back,
Can only go forward.

Comes the time,
When fighting the inevitable
Is no longer an option,
Resolve changes, time halts.

Time falters,
Time stops,
Time gasps,
Time resumes.

A pinprick of hope
Stares back and beckons,
Anger stirs and will
Forces a new resolve,
A new line of thought.

Back straightens,
Chin raises,
And a smile
Alights the lips.

Heart starts to sing,
Blood starts and rocks along,
Kerchuff, kerchuff, kerchuff, kerchuff.

Faster, faster,
Merrier, merrier,
Dancing with glee,
And gratitude.

Relaxing

Curling up
Warm and snug
Legs tucked beneath
A cosy blanket
A soft refrain
Drifting by receptive ears
Eyelids drooping
To flushed cheeks
A mouth curved at the edges.

Head back upon a cushion
Crackling fire in the hearth
Cat balled up on the lap
Dog snoring on the floor.

Sigh of ecstasy
Escapes the lips
As time passes
With no demands.

Relaxing

At last.

Ring of Fire

Within
Lies a maelstrom
Of roiling confusion,
Of emotional upheaval.

But that's
Just the surface.

Like the earth's crust
Hides a depth
Of molten rock.

But within the shell,
Unlike the soft lava
Middle of the earth

Lies nothing.

Not a hole
Not a blackness
But a brooding
Unrelenting chamber
Of non-existence

Within today's
Understanding.

But what of tomorrow?

Will it still be the same?

Mosaic

Or will some monster
More horrible than
The surface crust
Of life

Crawl out
Ready to devour
Everything in its path?

Or will the darkness
Turn to light
Bright enough
To eradicate the
Cacophony of feelings and ideas
Surrounding it?

Strong enough
To lift up life,
To break free
Of the constraints,
The limits,
The fears,
The pretences

That have kept
Bindings in place
Way past their use-by date.

You know, I'm rooting for Option 2.

Fearsome Creatures

Thump in the dark,
Scrapes on the wall,
Bumps in the closet,
Making skin crawl.

Shadows bizarre,
Moving this way and that,
Reaching with claws,
So hairy and fat.

Slithers across the floor,
Slime beneath the feet,
Time to jump into bed,
And cower under the sheet.

Hair on the arms
Stands up in fright,
Shivers down the spine
Each and every night.

Teeth set to chatter,
Convinced it's the end,
Eyes squeezed shut,
Prayers said to amend.

Creak goes the door,
Body hugged tighter,
As light from the hall,
Makes bedroom much lighter.

Mosaic

They're here,
Yes, they are,
Just outside the bed,
It's all over now,
We're all of us dead.

Quieting the screeches,
As a huge hand reaches
Down to the sheet,
And pulls it back, just a little,
Releasing warm heat.

The icy air invades,
That has come into the room,
And arms clutch the body,
And eyes peer into the gloom.

'Goodnight, little man,'
'Sleep tight if you can,'
'We're here, just next door,'
'And we couldn't love you more.'

All at once the creatures flee,
No longer able to hurt me,
I sigh and relax and look to the door,
Mum and Dad have made sure
I've nothing to fear anymore.

It's time

It's time
To get real
To get realistic.

To do what needs
To be done.

It's time
To know
What has to be known.

To know what needs
To be known.

It's time
To make changes,
To things that need changing.

To change what needs
To be changed.

It's time
To get better
To be better
To be the best
That can be

Or consequences dire.

Miracle

The universe
Rolls over
And a miracle
Is born.

Just when it is needed.

Fear clutches
At the breast
When the unknown
Descends

The miracle lights the sky
Until the reason for the fear
Is destroyed
And peace takes its place

Just when it is needed

Miracles
A way of life
When belief, need and patience
Lead the way

When the universe and God
Are one
And they agree

It is time
It is needed.

They Call Me Numbat

I am a banded anteater
'Numbat' is my name
I love to eat fat termites
And I'm cute and fast and game.

You see, I'm really very small
A marsupial with no pouch
I'm barely eight short inches tall
And I much prefer to crouch.

I have a long and bushy tail
Just like a bottle brush
I love to hold it way up high
To keep it clean and plush.

My tongue is long and thin and slick
My fur a stripey brown
I've two small ears upon my head
And my bottom's tough and round.

I work and travel in the day
And sleep right through the night
My home's a cosy hollow log
Where I jamb myself in tight.

I hate cats, and mangy dogs too
They chase me every day
Until I bare my teeth
To scare them all away.

Mosaic

W.A. is my favourite place
And they like me a lot here, too
I am their mammal emblem
And have pride of place in their zoo.

I'm sleepy now that night has come
I'd best be heading home
I hope to see you pretty soon
If around this way you roam.

Midnight

Stars
Masked with clouds
Hide the time
Of the night.

At night owls
Hoot
Softly
And mice scuttle off.

In the dark
Of the night
At the end
Of the day

Lies the border
Between today
And tomorrow

Some call it midnight.
To witches it's
Their time
When power
Spreads like blossoms
On the wind

And the will
Is easily swayed
When evil
Tendrils out
But good
Breaks its grip.

Mosaic

As the magic
Of midnight
Battles long
Battles hard

We mere mortals
Sleep soundly
Unaware
That another world

Exists that does
Not involve us
But could easily
Crush us.

If good did not prevail.

But goodness always does.

And goodness always will.

So we can continue
To sleep soundly
As midnight approaches
As midnight passes

As midnight nestles
Around us
And keeps us safe

For midnight is the ruling power.

Child of Mine

She's nineteen now
An adult
Responsible for herself
Her actions
Her life.

"But she's lost!"

No, she's looking
For something
For herself
For her way to live.

"It's not yours!"

No, it's not
It's hers
Her time to call the shots
Her way to live her life.

"Time's running out!"

Is it? Really?
She's only nineteen
She has plenty of time
She has me.

She will find herself.

When the time is right.

Trust the universe.
It's bigger than I am.
And just a touch older, too.

Devil's Edge

Darkness beckons,
Its teeth sharp and menacing,
Its allure unforgiving,
Uncompromising.

Thoughts where thoughts
Should not be
Emerge and clutch
With constriction
At the unwilling soul.

Night is the enemy,
Lying in wait,
Ready to pounce,
To drive its point home,
Into a heart already shredded.

A pitchfork of pain
Drives deep,
And connects
With the core of the being.

The devil
Lives
Within.

Unbeckoned.

And,
With toothless grin,
It claims its right to residence.

Energy

No more sparks
No more power
No more anything

Nothing but darkness
Nothing but numbness
Nothing but nothing

Only
Longing
Longing to be free
Longing to be me

Wanting no more shackles
Wanting dreams to progress
Wanting goals to be reached
Wanting desires to be met

Right now
No idea how
Changes that are needed
Can be made
Or how freedom can be reached

There's too much fear

To be Me.

Misty

Hiding behind the mist
Is who knows what?
But surely much is hidden there.

Standing on the edge
Watching, waiting, listening
Wondering what could be there.

Feverish in my ignorance
Hungry for the riddle's answer
But fearful of what might be there

Touching the mist before me
Plunging through the veil of mystery
To see for myself what is there.

Finding the courage to explore
Beyond the edge of misty reason
To seek that which is there.

That which all of us seek
That all of us need and want
That all of us must have

A conviction to be who we are.

No Explanation

Amongst the threads
Strides misunderstanding
Wishes
Turning to mud

Miracles
Become four-letter words
Masquerading
As kindness

Time
Does not take
Hope
Into consideration

Not when life
Barks
Orders
At empty space

Within the mist
Lies heads in hands
Honour in shreds
At the feet

Of more than injustice

Where no one
Deserves a right
To live

Everything ceases to exist.

Glimpses

Pressing down
In an effort
To contain

A world
Beyond understanding

A world
Leaking with vengeance

A world
Not of my making

Bubbling up
Escaping from control
Threatening to overwhelm

A thread of sanity
Clinging to

A stubborn inconsistency
Gripping

Desperately
To what is left

Glimmers of future
Bright and dull
Flash chaotically

Confusion comes
Along with pain

Hope sneaks a look
Sadness beckons

Guilt flashes past
Bitterness reigns.

For now.

Powerball

Tonight,
Sees the end
Of poverty.

Of wanting
To do more
Than the depths
Of my pocket

And time
Will allow.

Tomorrow,
Plans will be made,
And retirement begins.

Commitments will be met,
But it's time
For life to morph,
Yet again.

It is time for beginnings
To begin
And *this* –
To end.

Thank you, Powerball,
For making all this happen.

So I can shed happiness
To all I know.

Recollections

Sitting in a circle,
Bottle spinning,
Pointing to a sloppy kiss.

Trailing down
A sand dirt road,
On a hot sunny
Summer's day,
A willy willy
Chasing and stinging
Backs of legs.

A hazy face
Peering over the side
Of a cot,
Perhaps filled with sadness?
Hard to say.

A visit to Kew Cottages
To visit an inmate cousin,
Always a delight.

But then, sadly, he passed away.

No more Kew Cottage visits,
No more days of summer idling away,
No more heart skipping anticipation at spin the bottle.

But always wondering whether the face
Full of sadness was real.

Crystal Ball

Within the swirling
Depths of time
Amongst the mines
Dark and dim
Lie the answers

There are always answers

Twirling in ever
Wilder patterns
For anyone to see
To use as they wish
Lies the wisdom

There is always wisdom

When fear clutches
And palms grow slick
When the fog descends
To obscure all truths
Take heart that all will change

There is always change

Take heed of all you know
Of all you are and can be
Take heed to grow and learn
All that you need to know
For knowledge is power

There is always knowledge

Knowledge
Change
Wisdom
Answers

Life

Swirling in ever faster spirals
Coloured with disbelief
Fortified with acceptance
Made peaceful with inevitability

Made strong with unknowing
As we stride
Into the shrouding
Mists of time

To meet adventures

Yet to be revealed.

Philosophy

Dappled sunshine
Waning in the wind
Mixing shadows
In the afterthought of time.

Drifting through
The dust motes
Weaving through the web
As time does what time does.

Passes...

Afternoons dance with the prospects
Of mornings,
Which yearn for the moonbeams
Of Night.

No one can see
The time as it passes,
Poking out its tongue,
And waggling its years.

Mocking.

No one, that is
Unless
Time stands still,
Ceases to exist,
And then everything
Would happen at
Once,
In a rush,
On top of itself.

And time would no longer be.
Life would no longer be.

Nothing would be here.

If anything ever was.

Sleepy Head

Clutter clatters my bedroom,
Every inch covered by whims
And dreams flit up and over
Filling up nighttime to its brim.

I snuggle beneath my doona
Cuddling up close to something warm
As I bring my head within my pillow
To sleep beyond the dawn.

To sleep away in adventure
In times so bold and great
Playing in my imagination
Letting my stories determine my fate.

In the lands of my imaginings
I can be anything I desire
A damsel in distress
My knight battling dragon's fire.

Or even a dinosaur
Stomping through the brush
Or a whirlwind blowing hot and cold
Always travelling in a rush.

I can be awfully bad
Or terribly good
I can be as small as an ant
Or the tallest tree in the wood.

All while I sleep
The nighttime hours away
Allowing my mind
Its freedom to play.

Then when I awake
After dawn's brought its light
I feel all refreshed
From my adventures all night.

I can turn to my day
No matter how humdrum it is
Knowing tonight will bring
More crack, popple and fizz.

The Locker Door

I open my locker door
        Maths book stares
At me
        I peak around my
Open locker door

He's there
        Just as he always is
Laughing
        He disappears
Behind his open locker door.

I reach in
        Grab a book
Look around again
        And there he is
Beside my open locker door.

He sneers
        I slam my open locker door
Turn and flee.

I look back
        He is laughing
Again
        His eyes sparkling, bitter
As he leans beside my closed locker door.

I don't dare
        Return to my closed locker door
To exchange my English book for my Maths.

My maths book is laughing
        Behind my locker door.

The Wind

It whistles past my bedside
Like an old pot belly kettle
Preparing to blow its seams
As it rises, then falls to settle.

It drifts softly over my face
As I sleep all flushed and warm
Fanning the dreams within
Before the lifting light of dawn.

The clothes upon the clothesline
Are buffeted north and south
As the wind shouts upon their dampness
From its loud and howling mouth.

It's seen things us mere mortals
Could never begin to understand
As it travels fast and surely
Across the surface of our land.

It keeps our secrets close within
But its ghosts are well aware
That everywhere it travels
It takes away its share.

It whispers as it passes
It roars when life is wrong
It causes havoc at times of need
To test the very strong.

The wind is always present
Even when the air is still
It's then that it is gathering
It's strength to climb the hill.

The wind is fresh and ancient
It has no beginning, it has no end
It will go on ever after
Even past us women and men.

Enjoy it while you can
For you won't be here for long
Listen to the whispers
That are held in the true wind song.

Haze

Blurred existence
Surrounding
Pools of certainty.

Circling hope
Believing
In trust.

Warning signs
Flashing
Amidst the cerulean heights.

Nose twitching
At the sounds
Of silence.

Fog dripping
Off branches
Of daylight.

Stretching
Into never

Reaching beyond
The stars

Into the haze
Of tomorrow.

Finding the Future

Chasing rainbows
When time stands still
Finding answers
Climbing slowly up the hill.

Crossing out the t's
And dotting atop the I's
Wondering all the time
Is this all that hard work buys.

Casting out to sea
In a boat made from holey wood
Baiting out the hopes
As fast as this mystery could.

Crystal ball, o where art thou?
To mirror what will be
In the years that lie ahead
What can your true eyes see?

Will failure come a'knocking
Upon this fragile door?
Or will all turn out exactly
As this imagination so boldly saw?

Can't you peel back the wonder
Just a little bit
So what can be expected
Will be a perfectly good fit?

Mosaic

Without the drama, the hair pulling
The stress of working hard,
What is to be, what can be done
In the shed down in the yard.

To know if ambition
Is bigger than desire
And if the future holds anything
That will throw all into the mire.

Or will it be a joy
Something wonderful to behold
Just to have some knowledge
To have a destiny unfold.

Now that would be a wonder
Either way would be okay
Because then there'd be a reason
To wake and get up every day.

It's hard now to live enthused
For the life chosen on the spur
So just a little crumb of knowledge
Would help life's gears to purr.

Fingers crossed, lucky clover laid near
A foot beneath the pillow tonight
All will be helping to find the truth
Of the unknown future in near sight.

It's time to write the future
To make it what we need
To stir in the mix of want
To finally take the lead

So no more chasing rainbows
No more standing still
Instead we'll find the answers
And climb firmly up the hill.

We'll greet the hurdles straight on
We'll solve the problems too
And then we'll have a future
With a warm and glorious view.

Sunshine

It gleams
And dances
It lights up the world
It warms the senses

It is sunshine

It blinds
As it beams
Off metalwork
Into eyes unshielded

It is life

It burns
Skin exposed
Bare to the elements
The body working, sweating

Under a cloudless sky

It cheers
The heart
Empty and alone
Lifting the spirit

Giving meaning

It is warmth
It is energy
It is the beginning

It is sunshine.

Starbright

In the black abyss of time
Where only the past is highlighted in words
And the future remains beyond our grasp
We live our lives.

In the black abyss of time
Knowledge is gained day by day
Giving us hope that all will be right
To live our lives.

In the black abyss of time
There is no foreknowledge of what lies ahead
There is only mystery to explore
As we live our lives.

Within the black abyss of time
As we live our lives
Unfolds the joy of discovery
Like the stars in the night sky above.

First one light appears and then another
Until the true picture of our lives
Is linked like dots on a page
Forming the path our true heart must follow.

In the black abyss of time
All is revealed, all is possible.
If we just allow ourselves to believe
We can live our lives
The way we were meant to.

Springlike

Through the window
He seems to look at me
Head cocked to one side
I wonder whether he can see

Me looking at him
On the other side
Beyond the curtain
I wonder whether I should hide.

So that I might watch
My magnificent black and white
Bird as he lands gleefully
Upon the cushion to bite

A mouthful of the soft
Inner fabric, to create
A nest of brilliance
For his waiting, anxious mate

He digs his beak
Deep within the fibrous folds
And emerges with a mouthful
Of the forgotten fluff and holds

It tight as his beak
Descends again to take
Yet another bite
Until his beak is full to make

His nest the best
Nest in the neighbourhood
And then satisfied
He hops off to make good

The promise he's made
To his wife to provide
For the family soon to come
In a place secure where they can hide

Their young until
It is time for them to be
Able to show their colours
Without fear of being free

A heavy responsibility
But one joyously embraced
I can see it as he perches
And rests a little within his haste

He flies off east
I know not where
To deposit his burden
Amongst the other pieces of cushion hair

His nest must now soon be done
His toil has lasted so long
Spring is here and the air
Is sweetly filled with bird song.

Time Jumping

Where has it gone?

It was there.

I saw it.

I did it.

But now it's not.

The thought
Solidifies
As I reach
Out and redo
What I know I've already done.

How can that be?

I walk out the door
To an unexpected place.
I'm no longer at home,
In spring.
But on a mountain top,
In winter.

My clothes are not the same.
I'm wearing fur from
The insides of my shoes
To the brim around my hat.

I've been here before.
I made a snowman
On that slope
Yesterday.
But now it's gone.
Why is it not there?

Tingling runs across
My skin,
Almost déjà vu,
But I know
That I'm yet
To do these things
I think I've done.

The things I am
Doing right now instead
Of them already being
Done
As I recall them.

But the recollections
Slip away,
Too easily,
Too quickly

And confusion
Is the only thing
I'm certain of.

When time keeps jumping.

Wizard Fire

A click of the finger
The fire begins
The pot filled
With wonders.

What to magic?
What to begin?

Steam rises
From the brim of the pot.

A rainbow of kaleidoscopic colours
Twisting, dancing, smirking.

They add a pinch of candle wick
Followed by the wart from a hog.
Quickly after an anteater's eyebrow
Hops reluctantly into the brew.

The eyes of a blind rat
Milky and blank
Roll around in the
Mix of the cauldron.

Bat's ears, butterfly wings
And a hundred others
Are tossed and stirred
Within.

Until finally a word is said
To make the brew a potion
'Fire', says the wizard
And flames shoot up.

Their purple brilliance
Beautiful, bountiful, bewitching.

As the brightness fades
The wizard gathers it close.

Bottled and secured
It awaits its destiny
High on a shelf
Out of harm's reach.

The glint in the glass eye
Expectant and eager
Joyful and excited
Angelic and evil.

This wizard fire
Awaits its master.

Procrastination

Putting off what shouldn't be put off
Rendering time meaningless
Opening the doors to stress
Creating unnecessary problems
Reacting irrationally to what must be
Acting foolishly at times of need
Starting a destructive chain of events
Taking time out when time is not there
Initiating an emotional breakdown
Not accepting the inevitable
All the while knowing the consequences
Telling yourself there's plenty of time
Ignoring responsibilities
Organising, documenting, delaying
Needlessly, uselessly, irresponsibly

Such is procrastination
Procrastination is life

Wake up
And small the daisies

A good sneeze will get you moving.

The Sign

When riches become ashes
Life trains us to accept
Not only the circumstances
But who and what we are.

I'm still learning
And know that will go on
Until I die.
But I'm hopeful

That before then
I will become
Who and what
I am supposed to be.

Some believe there is no god
No universal power guiding
Our lives
Encouraging us to fulfil a greater pattern.

Some believe that everyone
Has a place in the jigsaw of life
A place that is pre-ordained
And linked to every other being –
Anywhere.

I fall into the latter category
But I am not good at reading
The signs left for me
And so it is taking me longer than others
But one day,
And I hope soon.

THE SIGN will come.

The Short Straw

The short straw keeps
Finding me

Keeps trying
To beat me

Keeps sticking
It's sharp ends

Into the woollen jumper
Of my life

Leaving pin pricks
Of blood

And trails
Of heartache

As it tries to satisfy
Its own needs

Its own wants

Its own cravings

With nary a thought
For anyone or anything else

But it never wins!

Night Time

Night pours from the sky,
Lit by a lazy moon,
A sliver only,
And then hundreds of
Thousands of LED lights spark
Too far away to be effective.

Traffic thunders dimly
In the distance,
A constant thrum
Of indistinguishable sound,
Leaking around the edges
Of hearing, trying not to.

The breeze through the cracked open window
Fingers through the room,
Brushing gently across the surface
Of the contents,
Filling the air and leaking
Through the fissures into the rest of the house.

Night wraps around everything,
Revealing nothing in its cocoon,
It steals dreams, creates nightmares
And it dies
At the first hint of day,
When dawn nudges it aside
And morning springs from its bed.

To light the corners of everyone's day.

Perception

When everything whirls
Around you
When the sky darkens
And the clouds argue.

When breathing
Seems too difficult
To achieve

And time
Runs life altogether.

When the birds
Sit silent in their trees
When dogs barking
Ceases

When the cats
Hide under the cushions
And their purring
Freezes in their throats

You can be forgiven
If you think
Something horrific
Is in the wind

When music is nothing
But discord and disharmony
When the sun's rays
Bring nothing
But pain and sadness.

When laughter
Haunts you until
You can stand it no longer
The joke not funny at all.

When the truth is empty
Unfulfilling

When the wind whispers
Terrible somethings
In your ear
As it travels past

Taking some of your soul
With it.

When living life
Seems like too much
Hard work
For no reward

It's time to stop
Thinking forward
It's time to let
Life in under your skin
To embrace it
To squeeze the joy from it

To live

To perceive it as it really is.

Conviction

Conviction lies in the truth
Of Certainty.

Tis one thing to speak
Something
But belief
Is entirely
Harder.

But, oh so much
More rewarding.

Saying
Has emptiness attached.
Hollow spaces between
The words.

Conviction
Belief
Oozes with warmth.

There are no holes
Where doubts can form.

Just a firm knowing
That nothing
Can change what is meant to be.

With conviction lies acceptance

And peace.

Bonfire

Sparks shoot upwards
Spreading ever wider
As the winds of time
Wander through the stream.

Old chairs,
Old fences,
Cardboard boxes, wooden toys,
All are sent in joy
To meet their maker.

Taking the memories
Of better times,
With them.

Couples huddle
Together,
Whispering of deeds
They'll do on their return
Home.

Children laugh and play,
With ever watchful
Parents delighting in their joy.

And on the edge
Of their existence
Stand I

Alone but lit with warmth.

Floating

The air is clear up here
Floating
Gently caressing the hair
From my face

Lightly feathering
Coolness
As it spreads about me

Floating

Thoughts drift away
Idly I reach out
To touch them

But they playfully
Slip beyond my reach

Floating

Away

Towards the grey horizon
Where on orange
Newborn sun
Peaks above the horizon

Floating

On the promise
Of a new day
A new way
Of life, of living

Floating

Seemingly aimlessly
Unattached to reality
Neither pushing towards
Nor pulling away

Just floating

Awaiting what there is to come

Awaiting whatever is in store

Awaiting the outcome of

Floating.

The Bench

Yellow leaves encrust the ground,
Hiding the earth beneath,
Raindrops run down the outside window,
Leaving trails of memories in their wake.

The branches of the elm tree sigh,
Upon the roof the rain taps down,
And all the birds huddle in the cold,
Watching the dull grey sky surround them.

Memories of better times, sunny times,
Flood their minds and hearts,
Until the rain comes not from the sky,
But from the eyes of a million little wrens.

Beneath the branches of the trees,
Sits a faded blue park bench,
Upon the bench sits a figure,
Hunched, alone, unaware.

The wrens watch as the rain,
Falls not from the sky,
But from the tightly closed eyes,
Of the figure upon the bench.

The grey sky turns to black,
The rain keeps tapping on the roof,
The birds keep huddling together,
The figure is still hunched.

The morning comes and the figure,
Sits still, hunched and alone,
The wrens watch and wait,
The rain passes and the sun shines.

The figure on the bench is still,
Until two people arrive,
Place the figure on a stretcher,
And take the figure away.

The wrens unwrap their wings,
Display them to the air,
And rise as one from their branches,
Going where the wind takes the soul.

Changes

They're always there
Knocking at our door
Seemingly needed
But sometimes what for?

At times when we least
Expect change to be
It will knock us off our feet
Before we have a chance to see.

Sometimes change is good
But sometimes it is bad
Sometimes it depends
On the sort of day you've had.

There's one thing for certain
In this fickle life we lead
That change will always be there
No matter what we heed.

It's best just to relax
And let it all just roll
That way life will be happier
And much easier to reach your goal.

You don't want to be fighting
Every minute of every day
Life wasn't meant to be so hard
Not in that meaningless way.

Drip

Drip
Drip
Drip
The walls have no doors
Have no windows.

Drip
Drip
Drip
The heart shrivelled
The life gone.

Drip
Drip
Drip
Senseless meaning
Senseless dreaming.

Drip
Drip
Drip
No place of feeling
Of belonging.

Drip
Drip
Drip
The sigh escapes
The breath releases.

Mosaic

Drip
Drip
Drip
When beginnings
Have no endings.

Drip
Drip
Drip
When endings
Are the beginning.

But of what?

Watching Time

The snow is spread
Upon the late winter turf,
Sunlight warms the surface,
A shoot, bent and determined
Pushes relentlessly through,
It straightens and reaches
For the warmth of the sun,
It spreads and it grows,
Turning its face upwards,
Smiling at the passersby,
Leaves spread along its stems,
Buds form,
At first tightly closed,
Protected by the greenery,
Staying close to the security
Of home,
But then gradually,
The sun beckons,
And the flowers
Crave the warmth
And brightness,
And the petals open
And embrace the world,
Hesitantly at first,
But then more boldly,
As they experience more,
And understand more
With less fear,

Mosaic

And then one day,
They spread even further,
And the wind takes them,
And they drift joyously,
Away to see more and be more.

But they always remember
The love and the nurturing
That made all this possible.

Musical Life

Sometimes
The song of life
Creates music within.

A music that blends
Harmony with existence
Where no discord
Is heard.

Sometimes the clarity
Of tone in life
Flows about and all around
Filling the senses to overfull
Until the heart of song evolves

Into a lyrical mosaic
Of melody filled with emotion
And experiences of a wondrous kind
Bursting forth into a crescendo
Of ultimate symmetry
And a decrescendo of fulfilment.

Such is the music of life

Love

And existence.

Mosaic

Tiny fragments
Of this
And that

Some good
Some bad
Some happy
Some sad
Some comical
Some fantastic
Some frightening
Some heroic

All joined
By a bond
Of being

Fragments of time
Fragments of moments
Fragments of joy
Fragments of peace
Fragments of love
Fragments of hate
Fragments of wisdom
Fragments of mistakes

All filled
With knowledge
Of existence

This makes up our souls
This makes up our lives

This is what being human is.

The Author

Pam lives in Seymour, Victoria, Australia with her two children and two cats.

She fills her days with writing, editing, proofreading, and publishing, which keeps her quite busy.

She loves to read, go to the movies, paint and play the clarinet. And, occasionally, she makes teddy bears.

Apart from poetry, Pam also loves to write fantasy novels for both young adults and adults. Often there is a sprinkling of romance in there as well.

Pam has also dabbled with children's writing, both picture and chapter books. She plans to publish these one day through her business – TB Books.

Other Books by Pam Collings

Kaleidoscope: A collection

ISBN 978-0-9871238-3-1 (paperbook)
ISBN 978-0-9923002-2-7 (e-book)

Soon to be released:

Practical Proofreading –
Tips, Tricks & Exercises
ISBN 978-0-9923002-1-0

All you need to know about the art of proofreading.
If you have ever thought about proofreading, maybe because you love to read and believe you have an eye for detail, then this book will help you to develop the skills necessary to break into this field.

Good luck!

www.ingramcontent.com/pod-product-compliance
Lightning Source LLC
Chambersburg PA
CBHW020426010526
44118CB00010B/447